Everywhere I Find Myself

Everywhere I Find Myself

Leah Stenson

Turning Point

Copyright © 2017 by Leah Stenson

Cover image: "Petite Dejuner" by Aimee Erickson
Typsetting: Robert Thieman

Published by Turning Point
P.O. Box 541106
Cincinnati, OH 45254-1106

ISBN: 9781625492500

Poetry Editor: Kevin Walzer
Business Editor: Lori Jareo

Visit us on the web at: www.turningpointbooks.com

୧ ୧ ୧ ୧ ୧ ୧

Acknowledgments

"At the Balch Hotel"—*Tiger's Eye*

"Beyond Reach"—*VoiceCatcher*

"Celestial Navigation" & "Ginza"—*Just Now: 20 New Portland Poets*

"Cross-Cultural Calligraphy," "Mystical Body," "Street Theater" & "Touched"—*Oregon Literary Review*

"Crossing"—*Motionless from the Iron Bridge: A Northwest Anthology of Bridge Poems*

"Flying to Ohio"—*Red Poppy Review*

"For My Poet Friends in Fukushima"—*Heiwa wo towa ni Kokoro ni Kizamu: 305 Shinjin Shu*

"Give It to Me Straight"—*Verseweavers*

"In Flight"—*Plein Air 2013 Anthology*, Columbia Center for the Arts

"In Lan Su Garden, the Garden of Awakening Orchids"—*2016 Multnomah Arts Center Poetry Pole, April selection*

"Inokashira Park"—*Sunset Liminal*

"Reboot"—*Fault Lines*

"Shabbas Goy"—*Raising Our Voices: An Anthology of Oregon Poets Against the War* (The Habit of Rainy Nights Press, 2003) & *Heiwa wo towa ni Kokoro ni Kizamu: 305 Shijin Shu*

"The Apple Doesn't Fall Far from the Tree"—*Cirque*

"Tokyo, the Floating World Adrift"—*Sacred Cow*

"Tokyo Trains"—*Colere*

"Two Views of Japan in Kawazu"—*Cloudbank*

"Untitled"—*Verseweavers*

With deep appreciation to Carl Adamshick for his encouragement and advice, and Bill Stenson, my most devoted fan, for his astute editorial comments and unflagging support.

For Emily and Marisa

Table of Contents

Flying to Ohio..17

Epic...18

Tokyo Trains..19

Give It to Me Straight..22

Ginza...23

Reboot...24

Arrhythmia..25

This *Saha* World..27

Aftermath..28

Healing Waters..30

Dreaming the Lotus Sutra..31

Inokashira Park..32

Rain Song..33

Untitled...34

Uncharted Waters..36

Compassion...37

Silence...38

Love Note..40

Reflection..41

Law of the Jungle..42

Two Views of Japan in Kawazu.....................................43

Artist's Statement..44

Cross-cultural Calligraphy ... 45

Street Theater ... 47

Crossing ... 48

Tokyo, the Floating World Adrift ... 49

In Lan Su Garden, the Garden of Awakening Orchids ... 51

Tao of Tea ... 53

Kotatsu ... 55

My Daughter Telephones Home ... 57

A Murder of Crows ... 58

At the Balch Hotel ... 60

Cosmopolitan ... 61

Touched ... 62

Neighbor Boy ... 64

Blueberry Picking ... 65

Words I Couldn't Say to My Mother ... 66

Beyond Reach ... 68

Tunisian Taxi Driver ... 69

Ode to Pillow Cases ... 71

While Leafing through *The City in Which I Love You* ... 73

The Apple Doesn't Fall Far from the Tree ... 75

A Chicken Soup *Mitsva* ... 76

Shabbas Goy ... 77

From a Number to a Name ... 78

For Nelson Mandela ... 79

For My Poet Friends in Fukushima ... 80

Little Lamb 82
Cows in Dufur 83
Best in Show, Dufur-style 84
Heart Throb 85
Parkdale 87
Birthday Eve on the Steel Bridge 88
Note to Self 89
In Flight 91
Celestial Navigation 93

I held fast to certainty, and when I let go, I saw I wasn't the only one going under. Luckily, I was buoyant and rose, braced myself for the next wave, and the next. After that first, all others seemed small by comparison, and now all of them comprise the narrative of my life, my art.

Portland, March 2017

Flying to Ohio

After a soporific of red wine and potato chips,
I drifted off over the Great Plains at midnight,
the cabin darkened, my heart and the heartland lit.

Now the sky is reddening in the east, and
in the west lights are clumped like islands
glimmering through velum.

On a solo adventure four decades ago, knapsack
on my back, I wandered from the foot of the Acropolis
to Delphi and Santorini, channeling light.

Returning home a prodigal wanderer, I never stopped.
Sometimes at high altitudes, I still find shards
of former selves, a polished stone, a sun-bleached shell.

Epic

Our family lived in a big house
where no one could connect.
The children's rooms were dim and in disarray.
You were distant and peripheral.
As I sat down with our daughter to draw a picture,
hundreds of moths came through the window.
In my dream, I crossed bridge after bridge alone.
Arabs on horseback by the side of the road
intoned a blessing to protect me on my journey.

Tokyo Trains

Pushed into rush-hour trains where windows
pop from pressure, impeccably groomed
salary men in white shirts and trench coats
read pornographic comics and sex ads while
shifting and lurching to the squeal of brakes.
They slyly rub up against pert little office ladies
in short skirts, hose and heels who will make copies
and serve tea in fluorescent, airless cubicles.
After work, these same salary men will go out
and drink until the last train and have to be held
as they stumble out the door of the *karaoke* bar
into the dark where they puke their guts out
on the train platform, waiting for the Yamanote line
to take them home to houses the size of rabbit hutches
where wives and children wait and pray
they won't come home too late or too drunk.

Saito-san is out in the rain tonight.
It is nearly midnight but his wife won't let him in.
He is calling her name and rapping on the glass door.
She, too, is drunk. In her house
there are no slippers in the *genkan*,
no *meshi* on the table, no hot water in the *ofuro*,

no covers turned down on the *futon*.
In other households, women wait patiently
for their samurai salary men,
the kamikaze of Japan's economic miracle.
They wait for men who are up too early
and home too late to see their children,
for men who come home stinking of sake,
who, after giving their lives for the company,
succumb to *karaoshi* (death from overwork),
or even worse, in their retirement, solidify
into *sodai gomi* (oversized pieces of garbage),
unwanted nuisances in their own homes.

The children fight their way into the trains through
bodies packed together as tightly as blades of grass.
Shouldering heavy leather knapsacks, they struggle
to carve out even a small breathing space.
Barely able to see over the heads of the commuters
to the concrete apartments and gray skies of the suburbs,
a blur beyond the windows dripping with condensation
and sweat, they brave the trains like little Spartans
in thin navy uniforms, in the dead of winter,
to attend the best schools, followed by cram
schools, until late in the evening. They study
to pass safely through the examination hells

that will open doors to the best universities
and then to the best companies, so that
they might follow in their fathers' footsteps.

Wives don't ride the trains much.
Only after preparing breakfast
and making *obento* for lunch,
after cleaning house and hanging
laundry, might some adventurous woman
take a train to somewhere. Most just bicycle
around town, children in the rear, groceries
in the front basket, babies on their backs,
stopping to gossip on the street with neighbors
as they make the ritual rounds to the fruit market,
fish market, post office and bank.
They might even drop by a friend's for tea.
But they don't want to go too far.
They have to be home to wait for their children,
to wait for the last train to bring their husbands home.

Give It to Me Straight

with a steady hand—
no twist,
just the terrible
exquisiteness of being
poured to the rim
of a whiskey glass,
neat.

Ginza

In the dim light of the cabaret
you soothe the sadness
of salary men with whiskey
and *karaoke* as you bow,
smile and serve up
an outpouring of welcomes
and compliments until
the money runs out.
Then, like a cold-hearted lover,
you offer no comfort to those
who can no longer afford you,
leaving them alone to leap
like lemmings onto train tracks
and be counted as *jinshinjiko*—
fatal body accidents.

Reboot

Unhook me
from the iPhone
the iPod
the iMac
the I.V.

Deliver me
from the iWork
the iWeb
the iWireless
the ICU.

Free me
from IT,
and the me
myself and I
the i, i, i.

Arrhythmia

Propped on a gurney in the ER,
my toenails poking out from under the sheet,
I'm glad I got a pedicure the day before.

Earlier I was the life of the party;
now I'm anxious, feeling down,
flat on my back in a surgical gown.

The woman in the bay to my left moans, and
to my right, a man is failing with a heart attack.
The doctor calls for intubation.

I implore my hubbie to never
let them intubate me! (Then
I wonder if I'll regret my plea.)

As the orderly wheels me to my room,
my rhythm not quite back, I ask
How's the man with the heart attack?

He says, *We don't know what happens
after they leave.* I feel lucky;
this time I got a reprieve.

This *Saha* World

My brother calls from Bridge Gardens on Peconic Bay. He's weeping, overcome by the beauty of it all. *It's like heaven*, he says, and mentions how much he misses our mother.

He hands the phone to our younger brother who tells me that his good friend is wasting away from cancer and won't stop drinking and smoking. She's refused his offerings of *konbucha* and apricot pits.

After I hang up, a friend calls to tell me she's decided to divorce the man she was head over heels in love with only last year. He's abusive.

I resist telling everyone they will be fine and their suffering will pass. I hold my words in check, instead listen carefully, trust my silence.

Aftermath

Poppi, this is your granddaughter
who you showered with money
and who you pinched on the cheek,
murmuring *Bella* whenever
I came to visit.

My love wasn't strong enough
to make you want to live.
Now, a half-century later, I'm still
trying to reach you, offering prayers
for the repose of your soul.

Abandoned by the fates,
you feared the recurrence of cancer
and spoke in a rasping whisper
no longer able to bellow
in anger and pain.

You didn't know
when you committed suicide
in your shiny new Cadillac
you would take Noni with you
to the underworld.

You couldn't imagine
you would leave me alone
to navigate a sea of suffering,
to spend half a lifetime
mining my darkness.

Healing Waters

Only yesterday, I saw you gliding someone across the therapy pool. I don't know you, but I think of you as a saint. You minister to the weak and infirm, some of whom must be lowered into the pool on a swing because they can't walk in on their own, like the woman who has no limbs at all. You look deeply into their eyes, the eyes of all of them, as you waltz them around in the warmth of the healing water. I imagine you are one of the few who touch them. You always look intent, serious, but suddenly you smile. Today I heard you're in the ER. If you don't come back, who will hold and guide them?

Dreaming the Lotus Sutra

The poet brought me a child.
As I held her, she directed my gaze
to a new galaxy, one so brilliant
it eclipsed the Milky Way, illuminating
a path to a new constellation,
lights numerous as the grains of sand
in the River Ganges.

Inokashira Park

Kichijoji, Tokyo

Circles on the rain-dimpled pond
expand, intersect, like kimono patterns.
Pitter-patter on a plastic umbrella
evokes memories of a nursery song
Japanese mothers sing to soothe
children house-bound on rainy days.
Pedestrians flow across a footbridge
past white swan paddle boats
huddled together at the water's edge.

I could dwell forever in this *ukiyoe*
moment, fragment of a floating world.

Rain Song

Words stream across the screen,
dark thoughts pool and swirl,
engulf me in the rising flow.

I start to go under as your poem surfaces,
the one that says *"you're not alone."*

I grasp it as I would a lifeline,
an urgency to create, solace
in the sound of rain.

Untitled

Dark and light were
in separate universes
along with the sun and moon
the stars and the night
the saints and the sinners
the living and the dead,
and beauty couldn't
coexist with ugliness
and love couldn't
coexist with hate.
And then, something opened
inside me, maybe when
they cut out my cancer
and left a scar the length
of my left breast.
Life came together then,
the good and the bad,
the pain and the pleasure,
the sadness and the joy.
I was no longer the same,
and I let it flow by
on the River Lethe
taking my sorrow out

into the depths

where it merged with the sea

of greater sorrow, making

my small sorrows smaller

until they were no longer necessary.

Uncharted Waters

I say to my mother as we dine
on filet of sole in a dimly lit
South Shore restaurant,
Your father killed your mother.

The company of witnesses,
wine and the neutral space
embolden me to span decades
of silence vast as the ocean.

My words, a rogue wave
plowing into a bridge,
take you out over your head
in their wake.

Struggling to regain your footing
you stab the air with your fork
and spew, *How dare you say that!*
You, the apple of his eye!

Compassion

Lounging on the deck
on a summer day,
I'm irritated when
My iPhone rings.

It's my mother calling to rail
against me and the world.
Instead of arguing with her,
I try lifting her spirits.

As if to reward a good cause,
a hummingbird flies up
just inches from my face,
its wings a tiny flutter of applause.

Silence

My father talked constantly
as if the sky would fall
if he didn't hold it up with sound.

My mother was often silent,
exuding calm before storms
of anger and disappointment.

So I spent decades
speaking torrents of words,
and when I was silent,
it was because I'd stuffed
them too deep inside
to get them out again
until a surgeon cut them out.

Only then did I learn to speak my truth
even when it was met with silence.
When I listen I can hear
my own words and, if I'm lucky,

the words of others,
even when their hearts are dark.

Love Note

I'm swept away
by your tropes,
similes, metaphors
and line breaks.
Can you find
room for me
in your white space?

Reflection

I lie at the edge of the pool, stare down
to the bottom. Reflections of overhanging
branches ripple in the evening chill.

Did he feel the chill before he took
that final dip, the dead man's float
in the pool in Vegas?

Was he on his back, gazing at the sky
when death overcame him? He was
facedown when they found him.

A shadow passes. I stare down
to the bottom of the pool.
Overhanging trees shiver and weep.

Law of the Jungle

My husband is fond of saying, *He who rides a tiger may never dismount.*

When he says this, he imagines he is the one riding the tiger and the tiger is his company. When I say it, I think I am the one doing the riding and he is the tiger. In any case, someone is riding and someone is ridden.

It's like that other thing he is fond of saying—about how all the animals in Africa start their day running: the gazelle to escape the lion, the lion to chase the gazelle.

I'm not sure what all of this means except to say that the world runs on power and someone is always on top, in the boardroom or bedroom, and many people get eaten alive, one way or the other.

Two Views of Japan in Kawazu

On the Izu Peninsula, Japan

The Resort

Hotel guests circle like sharks on the patio in anticipation of the lunch buffet. Hawaiian muzak drifts out over Sagami Bay where middle-aged surfers paddle about, waiting for a wave big enough to carry them to shore. The banquet doors are flung open and I'm swept forward with the crowd, behind three plump women in matching Aloha shirts who heap tsunami-sized portions of sushi, noodles, dumplings and sweets on their plates.

The Countryside

An old woman spreads seaweed out to dry on the embankment. A fisherman untangles his nets. A breeze rustles the bamboo by the side of the road. On the hill overlooking the sea, a farmer rests in the shade next to is hothouses of carnations and aromatic strawberries. We exchange greetings and he offers me an *amanatsu*—a tart, juicy summer orange, the taste of enlightenment.

Artist's Statement

This Chinese artist's brushwork leaves me
at a loss for words. Exquisite
cranes soar through gossamer clouds,
sampans float down tranquil rivers,
a perfect bird perches on a branch
of perfect plum blossoms in early spring.

His landscapes captivate me, especially
a fisherman at the foot of a mountain,
pole extending into the primordial mist.
Envious of his ability to transform
ink and paper into visual eloquence, I vow
to paint perfect poetic images.

I compliment the artist but my words
are met with stares and silence.
How arrogant, I think.
Again, I offer my tribute.
He smiles and points to a placard—
Thank you. I am deaf and mute.

Cross-cultural Calligraphy

I am the only Caucasian in a working class tea shop on the Bowery in New York City's Chinatown. A tiny stoop-shouldered Chinese grandmother takes the seat across from me. She places her tea and steaming rice-flour dumpling on the Formica table, points to my sesame ball—a deep-fried dough of glutinous rice stuffed with sweet bean paste and encrusted with sesame seeds—and gives me a thumbs-up.

She speaks in Chinese and points to the pastry case. We communicate our ages with hand gestures. I can write some Chinese characters, a benefit of having lived for many years in Japan. I write the character for person, then the characters for Japanese person and Chinese person. She excitedly gives me a thumbs-up and begins writing on her paper napkin.

She asks to see my right hand. She wants to read my fortune. She writes more characters on the napkin. I smile to show my appreciation. Next, she asks to see my left hand. She seems intent on communicating. *Tindola, tindola,* she repeats. I look puzzled so she reaches into her hand bag and pulls out a ten dollar bill. She wants me to pay for reading my fortune.

I point to my watch, present her with the bean cake I had wrapped for takeout, and head for the door. As I leave, I give her a big thumbs-up.

Street Theater

At the corner of Broome and Mulberry in New York City's Chinatown I sit with my window rolled up to block out the stench from black plastic garbage bags piled up at the curb. A plump pre-teen girl sits on a stoop eating Chinese moon cakes. A red truck roars up to the traffic light with a white van in pursuit. The guy in the van shouts *Fuck you!* over and over. The driver of the truck jumps from the cab, sticks out his butt, lowers his pants to the crack and spits back, *Go ahead. Fuck me. I dare, you!* The guy in the van leans full blast on his horn. The light changes and they speed off, tires screeching, rubber burning. Bystanders on the sidewalk applaud.

Crossing

Lifetime after lifetime
destiny mapped
in psychic filaments in
the firmament, causality
colliding with karma.
Speeding down the freeway,
certain of our destination,
we end up somewhere
unexpected, unable
to cross the bridge
leading us home.

Tokyo, the Floating World Adrift

Instead of Asian architecture with antique charm,
I found box-like concrete structures
built hastily after the war.
Ponds with footbridges were still to be found
yet few Japanese had time to sit in a garden,
much less admire the moon.
Women rushed about in drab business attire
elbowing their way onto the trains like samurai
salary men in their blue pin-striped suits.
People flocked to department stores with more fervor
than they did to places of worship.

The city of my dreams, long gone before I arrived,
had quaint tile-roofed houses and gardens
with wooden footbridges crossing koi ponds
where Basho's moon rippled on the water's surface.
Women in floral kimono tightly bound
with yards of satin obi encircling their waists
teetered on wooden geta, their hips swaying gently
as they minced along cobblestones on the way
to Shinto shrines and Buddhist temples

where incense graced the air and people intent
on purifying themselves intoned the sutra.

In Lan Su Garden, the Garden of Awakening Orchids

> *"You have associated with a friend in the orchid room and have become as straight as mugwort growing among hemp."*—The Writings of Nichiren Daishonin

In April, on the Buddha's birthday,
I sit with poets in the Scholar's Study
putting pen to paper with deliberation.

The light is perfect in late afternoon,
fretwork on windows and doors
transform courtyard foliage into art.

The world outside—blast of car horns,
squeal of brakes, passing train—
cannot distract me. I will it so.

One has only so many chances
in this lifetime
to write poetry in a garden.

Buddha spoke of good companions
in the orchid room. Exuding the fragrance
of happiness, I am here among them.

Tao of Tea

When my Chinese poet friend
comes for tea at my country house
I serve Tie Kuan Yin,
Iron Goddess Oolong.
It's lilac fragrance
and honey-smooth taste
stir the well of memory.

Looking at the little red tea tin
she tells me it's from Fujian Province
where she was born.

Reminiscing about the tea fields
of her childhood, she says
that after the tea is grown
farmers export it to the north.

Over our second cup
she reveals how
her family escaped
from the mainland,
leaving behind her baby brother.
Forty years would pass

before she saw him again.

Over our third cup, the tea
now a pale shade of gold,
she shares her belief
that her fortune came
from her timely birth
in the year of the horse.
As my friend is leaving
the neighbor's American Paint
appears, unfettered, grazing
sweet pea in my yard.

Kotatsu

A news photo shows a *kotatsu** littered with the remains of a family's last meal before fleeing the Fukushima nuclear disaster: Styrofoam containers of Cup Noodle, disposable chopsticks, plastic soy sauce bottle, a box of tissues and electric hot water pot—the detritus of modern Japanese life.

Months later, the family was allowed to return, but only for a few hours, to retrieve valuables, documents, clothing and keepsakes. Although it might be years before nuclear refugees can again inhabit this village, perhaps they take some small comfort in knowing their homes remain waiting for them, frozen in time like a modern-day Pompeii.

* *Kotatsu: A low table with an electric heating element underneath. People sit with their legs under the kotatsu for warmth.*

My Daughter Telephones Home

…from northeastern Japan where she's volunteering, digging in the mud six months after the tsunami. She thinks she's found a clump of human hair and is hopeful one more victim of the tsunami can now be identified and a spirit laid to rest. I worry about her doing such difficult work, remaining in a country still reeling from a tsunami and nuclear disaster.

When Marisa was a toddler, an older Japanese woman babysat her while I was at work. With Marisa on her back, Tsutsui-san weeded the grounds and mopped the floors of the dormitory I supervised—even though I never asked her for help.

She sometimes brought Marisa to her home, fed her sweet potatoes roasting on a kerosene stove and taught her to chant the Lotus Sutra. I wish Tsutsui-san could see how the lotus seeds she sowed took root and flowered in Marisa's heart.

A Murder of Crows

*Crows have settled
on a bare branch
autumn sunset.*—Basho

Crows rain-blackened and dripping
jeer from bare branches.

A chicken far from the hen house
picks its way along the hedge.

Crows caw like spectators
high in the cheap stadium seats.

A hawk swoops down
in pursuit of the chicken,

head now buried in the hedge,
legs and rump exposed.

The hawk scores.
The crowd goes wild.

The rump shudders and spasms
as a cloud of feathers forms,

floats down on hedge and grass,
settles like snow.

The hawk takes off.
Crows drop to the ground.
They feast on leftovers
at the after-party.

When the postman arrives
birds flee the scene.

At the Balch Hotel

A hotel that has seen better days, Dufur, Oregon

From my window at the Balch Hotel, I see cows coming over the hillside at a fast clip. *They are making time*, I say. You say, *They are making hay*. I notice how some have a calf in tow and you tell me how their sex is timed to give birth in the spring. I'm wondering whether they do it at other times, when you say, *It's not like the moon is full, the flowers fragrant, and they feel romantic.*

At breakfast you calculate how many people are orgasming around the world at any moment. By now we have forgotten about the cows. You compare me to a barroom Jezebel who might have taken a room in Dufur's heyday at the Balch with her outlaw cowboy. I liken you to Wild Bill, hoping tonight we'll shoot the lights out.

Cosmopolitan

The coat check man at MoMA greets me with a spirited *Komban wa*. I am surprised...until I remember I am wearing my T-shirt with the picture of a geisha drinking tea. *Komban wa. Ogenki desu ka?* I reply, assuming he speaks Japanese.

Instead, he asks, *Ca va?* I counter, *Bien. Comment allez vous?* I've nearly exhausted my French when he says something I don't understand. He pauses, then provides an English translation.

Russian. I am Russian, he declares. *How I love the sound of Russian*, I enthuse in English. I'm enjoying my repartee with this charming multi-linguist but people are waiting in line.

The coat check man smiles, hands me my overcoat and wishes me *dasvidanya*. With a burst of *je ne sais quoi* I bow my *sayonara* and high step out into the night.

Touched

Mr. Kim, a short but powerful Korean wearing a New York Yankees baseball cap, stretches my arm higher and higher until I feel like a crane taking flight. On the edge of pain, my body gives itself over to his powerful hands freeing my tendons from their adhesions.

He murmurs incantations in Korean as he works. A particularly painful spot brings tears to my eyes. *Does it hurt?* he asks. *Only in my mind*, I reply. He nods knowingly. *Yes, frozen shoulder. Too much pain.*

He bends my arm behind me and stretches it gently across my buttocks. *Good,* he says like a proud parent. *Today, two more inches this way.* Flexing and raising my arm and placing my hand behind my neck, he says with amusement, *Now you can wash neck.*

During my sessions with a physical therapist and acupuncturist, I joked how they could get jobs at Guantanamo. With Mr. Kim I don't feel like joking. *Praise God. Jesus loves you*, he exclaims at the conclusion of every session. I know it's true. Someone or something loves me because I've found Mr. Kim's healing hands.

You Christian? he asks on the day of my final treatment before I leave New York City to fly home. *No, Buddhist,* I reply, aware of the irony. *I pray, you pray,* he says, bringing his palms together, and I know it's not just lip service.

Neighbor Boy

At 16, Doug had the strength to lift me
onto the pile of sweet-smelling grass
in the compost bin behind his garage.

Unable to get out without his help,
I felt what it is was like to be stuck
in Peter Peter's pumpkin shell.

I worried about getting home before the rain,
and then about fire as Doug lit matches,
tossed them on the spongy, damp clippings.

I pleaded with him to help me down.
Only after he had struck all the matches
did he grip my arm, pull me toward him.

Like Georgie Porgie, he enraged me
with a kiss. Only then did he lift me,
set me on the ground again.

Blueberry Picking

One sunny summer morning in August, Noni suggests we go berry picking. I'm delighted because I had never been berry picking before, but feel some apprehension realizing that we'll be going into the woods so I ask, *Will we be okay? Are you sure we won't get lost?* Stroking my head, she reassures me, *Bring me your hairbrush and I'll braid your hair so you'll look like Pocahontas.*

I feel special since no one has ever braided my hair before. My mother sometimes brushes my hair into a ponytail, but she pulls it tight and it hurts. Noni brushes my hair gently and parts it down the middle. She divides each side into three sections and plaits them into neat braids secured with red rubber bands. I am transformed into a brave little Indian princess like the beautiful Pocahontas I saw in the Disney movie.

We set out carrying metal pails and I'm careful to stay close to Noni as we make our way through brambles and low-lying branches. Noni promises to bake me blueberry tarts when we get home, and the thought of having my very own little pie makes me indescribably happy.

Words I Couldn't Say to My Mother
Riverhead Hospital, Long Island, New York

Seeing you in the hospital bed,
tangled in the sheets,
I no longer feel the fear
you struck in my heart.

In childhood, I bound my sorrow
like a chrysalis in a sheet
wound of snow-colored silk
to soothe the inflicted wounds,
words that still smolder somewhere deep.

You would erupt with the fury
of an explosive volcano,
the sorrow of your agony
streaming down my cheeks like lava,
the taste of sorrow in my mouth,
your face, the mask of a raging fire
goddess burning a hole in my brain.

Now, small and stooped,
your eyes no longer smoldering,
your mouth no longer spewing fire,

you are simply you, and I
no longer fear who I am becoming.

You withdraw as I reach for you,
retracing a litany of my failings,
a trail of sorrows. It hurts not to say,

I love you, and, *I forgive you,*
to see you leaving me,
our mother-daughter bond
a brittle chrysalis hanging on
long after the frost,
the butterfly never taking wing.

Beyond Reach

Skin, thinner than paper,
could no longer contain
her bodily fluids
seeping into her deathbed.

We dare not embrace her.
Only the flesh of her
face could bear our touch.

Tunisian Taxi Driver

The first thing I noticed that June evening as my daughter Marisa walked towards me on 42nd Street in Manhattan was the red and white cotton scarf—a *keffiyeh**—wrapped around her shoulders. She explained that the *keffiyeh* was a present intended for *me*, given to her by a Tunisian taxi driver.

Back in December, we had hopped a cab in midtown Manhattan. When we discovered the driver was Tunisian, Marisa excitedly told him she had visited his country and wondered if he knew any of her friends. *Not possible*, was his retort. He was obviously in a bad mood and not very communicative. When he dropped us off, Marisa gave him a generous tip despite his frosty attitude. We were barely out of the cab before he floored it and sped off.

The night before I met Marisa in Manhattan she attended an opening at a SoHo gallery where she was introduced to a Tunisian named Becem. At first, Marisa couldn't place him, but he insisted he knew her. It turned out that Becem was the short-tempered taxi driver we'd encountered six months earlier.

He confessed he had felt hopeless that December night…ready to give up on life. My daughter's kindness had touched him. From the moment he sped away from the curb, he regretted his callousness. For days afterwards, he hoped and prayed he could somehow run into her again so he would have a chance to make amends. Although he professed to not believing in a God, Becem now felt that being able to meet Marisa again was proof the universe had answered his prayers. He took off his *keffiyeh* and wrapped it around Marisa's shoulders, asking her to give it to her mother as a token of his appreciation.

Standing on the corner in mid-town Manhattan as she related the tale of her encounter with Becem, Marisa removed the *keffiyeh* from her shoulders and wrapped it around me. With that simple gesture the past was altered and Marisa, Becem and I grew closer, cloaked in the solidarity of compassion.

* Keffiyeh have been worn by Arab men for centuries, but in recent years they have come to be associated with Arab solidarity, and the red and white keffiyeh, in particular, with radical Palestinian factions. In the West, Bohemians and hipsters have taken to wearing keffiyeh as a fashion statement.

Ode to Pillow Cases
After Pablo Neruda's "Ode to My Socks"

My daughter made me a pair of pillowcases for Christmas, sewn with her own sweet hands, of six-hundred-thread-count-cotton smooth as the River Nile. And when I lay my head down to sleep as though on a cloud profusely patterned with green fireflies and white daisies and pink blossoms against a background blue as a cloudless sky, I become an Egyptian Queen, and my husband, a Pharaoh.

These heavenly cases elegantly trimmed in burnt orange make me deliciously somnambulant, lull me gently into the night of the Technicolor dream world of my childhood or, sometimes, the lofty poetical dreams of Xanadu, and sometimes the mysteries of The Book of the Dead. I resist the urge to store them in their pristine state forever with my other treasures, lace and damask, in the cedar chest.

As children showcase glass menageries on shelves above their beds and adults their certificates of achievement on office walls, I restrain myself from displaying them behind non-reflective glass in frames of fine-grained fruitwood as testaments of daughterly love and motherly worthiness. Recklessly, I embrace my pillow enveloped in the grace of loving creation.

The moral of my ode is this: beauty is doubly beautiful when it is a matter of two pillow cases made of fine Egyptian cotton, purer than virgin wool, upon which two parental heads are dreaming.

While Leafing through *The City in Which I Love You*
New York City

Memory revises me.—Li-Young Lee

On a Saturday morning I sit in the Spring Street Cafe in Nolita watching young lovers. The woman speaks softly with graceful hand motions; her partner sits with elbows on the bistro table, fingers laced as if in prayer. They are a perfect counterpoint to the restaurant's décor: a Roman youth immortalized in marble, the form of a woman taking shape from a chunk of pink alabaster, two gold cherubs embracing.

An older couple at a neighboring table is lost in *The New York Times*. The woman repetitively twists a lock of hair around her finger; the man sits slouched in his seat. After finishing her coffee, the woman orders orange juice. I wonder if she wants time to linger, more time to connect.

But it's the young couple who spark my imagination, a kaleidoscope of nostalgic café scenes in New York, Tokyo, Athens, Paris.... If someone were to watch me, they would see a silver-haired woman alone with her cappuccino and croissant, scribbling in a little black notebook. The couples barely notice when my spoon slips off the saucer and clatters to the floor.

When the waiter approaches to ask if everything is OK or if I want anything more, I reply, *I'm fine. Everything is just perfect.*

The Apple Doesn't Fall Far from the Tree

One summer's day, my daughter phoned home from her art school in Greenwich Village. I mentioned that I was going blueberry picking. *What!? Why would you want do that?* She sounded concerned.

Because I want to have enough berries to put up for the winter, I replied, proud of myself at how far I had come in my development—from New York City to Tokyo and finally to the Oregon countryside. How disappointed I was in my daughter's big-city attitude!

Soon I set out for the berry fields. After a ten-minute drive down a one-lane country road, I couldn't find the turn-off and started to think that it was indeed a very hot day and there would probably be bugs on the berry bushes so I pulled over at the next farm stand and picked up a flat for twenty bucks.

In a New York-minute I had more than enough berries to last all winter.

A Chicken Soup *Mitsva*

I had been coughing and hacking into humanity's melting pot when my dear friend made me chicken soup. Lightly laced with dill, Lotus' broth had an Eastern European flavor. Carrots, celery, onion and chicken were the essentials in her elixir, as they are in any mother's soup, but Lotus' had something more: fluffy doughy puffs of matzoh, a kind of manna which, though it didn't cure me, comforted me and gave me strength.

Shabbas Goy

In a faded photograph, my father appears as a skinny boy with sunken eyes holding a cutout of a paper moon. A Gentile in a neighborhood of Jews, he lit the stoves for the faithful on Sabbath eves. During the war, the Nazis shot his plane down. He bailed out, his parachute becoming entangled in a tree, feet barely touching the ground.

They cut him down and threw him in a POW camp where he remained until the end of the war sending coded messages in letters and helping other prisoners escape, although as an intelligence officer he was duty-bound to remain behind. Daily rations were meager, mainly cereal infested with worms. One day, when his buddies bribed the guards for a chicken, he refused to eat it. In fact, he refused to eat chicken for the rest of his life.

From a Number to a Name

for Alter Wiener, Holocaust survivor

Nobility marks the face of this survivor
who refused to lose his way in the fog of war.
Number #64735 lives on into his eighties,
telling his story to those who gather
in schools, libraries, synagogues and churches,
to multitudes who will never forget his name.

Reaching out to touch his arm in gratitude,
I feel helpless, overcome by emotion.
His life inspires me to be better rather than bitter,
to be the change I want to see.
Don't cry, he says, with a gentle smile.
I've done enough of that for both of us.

For Nelson Mandela

After death, reverberations
of his actions for the good
imbue heaven with the kind
of illumination one finds
in a painting by Caravaggio,
light so divine its palpable
warmth dispels fear
of our mortality.

Surpassing the artistry
of any masterpiece,
this life in passing gives rise
to the presence of immortality,
creates in its departure
a vision that leaves us
awe struck, radiant
as the sky just after sunset.

For My Poet Friends in Fukushima

In requiems for the dead
and prayers for the living,
the voices of poets
rise and reverberate
from the wasteland
of Fukushima
defying a silence
broken only
by the caw of crows
and the clanging
of metal in the breeze.

On the winds of hope
their words arrive
on American soil.
Like seeds, their truth
will be sown in the hearts
of people who,
in a unified plea,
also speak against
the nuclear demon

that must be vanquished
to keep all people safe.

Little Lamb

In the spring pasture
sheltered by the flock,
you genuflect,
lips mussing the earth
as you nibble the grass.

Little Lamb, do you know
why you were born
or wherefore you go?

In the autumn chill
you'll come inside
dressed for dinner,
and all who gather
to feast will rejoice.

Cows in Dufur

At 8:00 a.m. the cows cross the apple green hillside,
a ribbon of black punctuated with dots of brown ocher.
Mother cows with their calves aim purposefully
for some unseen destination over the hill.
Going to work, you say.

Later that morning I deviate from my walk
around town to follow the bend in the road bordering
saffron-colored fields strewn with carcasses
of tractors, cars and scrap metal.

I find the cows penned in by electric blue barbed wire.
As I approach, some turn aside; others direct
their gaze right at me, skewing their heads,
switching their tales.

I lock eyes with a brown heifer, her pinkish beige
udder swollen with milk, her calf nuzzling at her side.
I envy her centeredness, her standing stock still.

Best in Show, Dufur-style

I'm walking down the street in Dufur when a reddish-brown dog with white patches bounds across the lawn to greet me. The owner hollers, *He's friendly!*

When I commend him for the dog's exemplary behavior of not jumping all over me, the big baby-faced fella with golden locks tells me how his Australian Heeler was sired by the same stud as George Strait's dog. *You know,* he says, *George Strait, the country singer whose famous song goes "All My Exes Come from Texas."* I say, *Sure,* telling a white lie.

He goes on about how the stud escaped from his pen when the breeder forgot to close the gate. I tell him that story is even better than having a dog with an honest-to-gosh pedigree and he beams from ear to ear.

Heart Throb

I'm sitting in a Greek deli,
hooked up to a heart monitor and
about to order a glass of table wine,
hoping it will induce arrhythmia.

The waiter reminds me of a poet
who gave me a rose in a cafe on Hydra
and told me I was on fire
after I emerged dripping
from a cold shower.

Now far from the Aegean,
I'm alone with my monitor,
feeling chilled by the air conditioning,
no longer warmed by the setting sun,
drinking Retsina and dining al fresco
with my paramour in a *taverna* by the harbor.

A young woman in a pencil skirt
slips into a seat at the next table.
She looks a lot like me when I was twenty.
I've been waiting to order,
but the waiter bypasses my table
and takes the younger woman's order first.

My heart skips a beat.

Parkdale

The sun sinks below the ridge.
The sky flames yellow and pink.
Breathing deeply, I sense lilac, feel
the warmth of your hand in mine.
Birds twitter, children play,
a dog barks in the distance.
From our deck, a raft
on a swell of boxwood,
we scan the distant pasture,
float into the fading light.

Birthday Eve on the Steel Bridge

Crossing the Willamette
I'm at the hub of my world.

The sky is crimson,
the city a jeweled silhouette.

Behind wisps of clouds
a super full moon rises.

I want to take a photo
but there's nowhere to stop.

Tomorrow I'll be a day older,
wiser, and full like the moon,

at home in the universe,
radiating my own little light.

Note to Self

The art of selfhood is an art to practice years before you no longer have the chance. It's not that you don't love people the way you used to. It's just that there's too much to say before you leave—too much to say about why you love them and why you don't, too much to say about places you've been and about places you still want to explore. And there's too much to say about who you were, who you are and who you want to become.

Of course, you must listen to people's complaints and sorrows (how parents, a spouse or society is to blame for this or that misfortune) but don't succumb to the notion that you are a savior, that you have power to save anyone other than yourself. Let go of your certainty; learn to breathe amid the rubble of edifices; steel yourself against wildfire; and when you slip beneath the waves, rise to brace yourself for the next wave and the next, the narrative of your life, your art.

Write your poems, paint your canvases, dance and sing until your self is ready to leave itself behind. Be where the trail leads to the mountain top, where new growth springs from scorched earth, where sun hides behind weeping clouds and dark sky, where thoughts swirl like whirlwinds or small tornadoes. Drop the stories and find an anchor, the beating of rain on a window, blood pulsing in your veins. Then you'll know you made the right choice about what you did with your time.

In Flight

The wind is a prayer,
sweeps the land clean
across this cliff high
above the river,
terrain where Icarus
might have taken flight
with all who aspire
to the zenith of the sun.

The Columbia below
wends its way, ready
to embrace the fallen,
the angels and the devils
who made their way
to this Edenic valley
after fire and ice
cleaved rock and floods
opened the way
for civilization.

The sun meets one halfway
on this stark plateau,
bleaches the tall grass,
casts an Aegean haze
over distant hills
cloaked in fir and pine.
Eternity can be heard
in the stir of the breeze
in the vineyards,
the whisper of prayer.

Celestial Navigation

While everyone slept,
I drove the family car
of my childhood
in the dark, circling
familiar neighborhoods.
The stars were bright
but I couldn't orient
to their light. Home
wasn't far away, but
the road never ended.

From light years away
my past takes the shape
of a new constellation.
I circle like a nighthawk
on the crest of the wind as
the magnetism of starlight
sweeps me up into blackness.

About the Author

After graduating with an M.A. in English Literature from State University of New York at Stony Brook, Leah Stenson worked as an assistant editor in New York City for Hawthorne Books and *School Library Journal*. She moved to Tokyo to pursue a spiritual quest to deepen her understanding of Buddhism and spent 16 years teaching English at a Japanese university and women's junior college. Upon returning to the United States, she served as managing director of Oregon Peace Institute while providing editorial assistance to the SGI Buddhist organization headquartered in Japan. She is an active member of her Buddhist community, serves on the board of Tavern Books and hosts the Studio Series, a monthly poetry reading and open mic.

Her poetry has appeared in literary journals such as *Oregon Literary Review*, *Cloudbank*, *Verseweavers*, *VoiceCatcher*, *Colere*, *San Diego Poetry Annual* and numerous other periodicals. Her chapbooks, *Heavenly Body* (2011) and *The Turquoise Bee and Other Love Poems* (2013) were published by Finishing Line Press. She served as a regional editor for *Alive at the Center: Contemporary Poems from the Pacific Northwest* (Ooligan Press, 2013) and as a co-editor with Asao Sarukawa Aroldi of *Reverberations from Fukushima: 50 Japanese Poets Speak Out* (Inkwater Press, 2014), an award-winning finalist in the "Social Change" category of the 2015 USA Best Book Awards.

Drawing on personal and cross-cultural experience, her narratives of everyday life explore the suffering and joy of the human condition and redemptive power of compassion. A world traveler, her poems have been translated into Japanese and Chinese. After many years of long-distance living, she feels thankful to be with her husband and two daughters in the Pacific Northwest.

Also by Leah Stenson

Poetry

Heavenly Body
The Turquoise Bee and Other Love Poems

Anthologies (co-editor)

Alive at the Center: Contemporary Poems from the Pacific Northwest
Reverberations from Fukushima: 50 Japanese Poets Speak Out

Made in the USA
Columbia, SC
01 November 2017